IS KNOT

John M. Bennett

Luna Bisonte Prods

2021

IS KNOT

© John M. Bennett 2021

Poems from June-October, 2016

Cover images & all other images © John M. Bennett 2016
 The Bennett art on back cover incorporates a small erasure text by Texas Fontanella.

Some of these poems first appeared in these fine venues, sometimes in slightly differing versions:
 Blank Sight/Naked Sunfish, DOC(K)S, Big Hammer, Fell Swoop, Otoliths, Utsanga, The Curly Mind, Haiku Canada Review, OPoetry, Marymark Press Give-Out Sheet Series, Zoomoozophone, Dada Centennial: Day of the Dead, Emozioni, and The In-Appropriated Press

Book Design by C. Mehrl Bennett

ISBN 9781938521744

www.johnmbennett.net
https://www.lulu.com/spotlight/lunabisonteprods

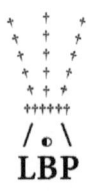

```
    *   *
   * * *
  *  *  *
   * * *
    ****
   / o \
    LBP
```

LUNA BISONTE PRODS
137 Leland Ave.
Columbus OH 43214 USA

loose the knot

the wallet sinking in a bathtub
is a mouth open on the word
if was *if* if gnats were
gathered on a cloud's open
lip the cloud churns
your laundry blown
across a lawn fire
flickers in a window open
on a word *off* stuck
inside your throat which
is a lake beneath the earth a
rope burning in reverse

if if if if if if if if if off
-John M. Bennett

itinorisifso

it it it it it it it it it
is
n't

in in in in in in in in in
un
der

or or or or or or or or or
er
go
ne

is is is is is is is is is
as
h

if if if if if if if if if
off
er

so so so so so so so so so
saw
n

meat expansion

where the hot wall dreams
is off the slower flame is
mud squirming in the d
rain your hand reached
for is cloud amino acid
framed against a wall a
truck swaying in the
freeway wind a nostril
clawed behind a mirror
your blood was numbered
useless leaking like a book

...leak and shine...
- F. Orklindt

full fool

fists and T orn

a me ant ● de
blistered

shiny b one

formic

comb
antant

X = X

)or less

heel haw

dust tom e
at's U or
wand ered

p a s t a s h o e

reburn

umbellical

~ ~ ~

embolition I

ccan't

orn

water a h
am or w ere

a glass a w ind

w w w w w w   w   w

C rate

tr eat sot
was **K**nife or
Stool

was table **I**s

caw

baw ble
k not
runn y 's
not de
doubled

◐ ●

coneojo

tu huevojo condens ata
me la piernaa más O
fulminado O fon ética
l ubrecada mi alfiler
enters the yolk of yr
eye ay intóónsico ,dual
butt *one* of the ddots
•))sieze the sleep detail(((

, *foggy rabbits chew the*
writ thing

...centro de la libertad de la lámpara
-Jorge Cáceres

fold

is an is
sue is
n't a ah
cor n o w ater
ccrawl th e arth

fill

fluted corn
man's lice
the hics'
nomantic

real s law

time

indecibel
incre ated
cr ash of f
wall ,moves

ins

time or f
licker it's
its nomen

flan ,fog

inbead

bulboid ddeck
infaucets

chain s *ink*

start

≈

lake

book tree *turd* tree book
tree book *lake* book tree
book tree *turd* tree book
tree book *lake* book tree
book tree *turd* tree book
tree book *lake* book tree
book tree *turd* tree book
turd book *tree* book turd
tree lake *turd* lake tree
book lake *tree* lake book
tree book *turd* book tree
lake book *tree* book lake

turd

tree

≈

≈

***Mantrafied in Ivan Argüelles'
"Kunst der Fuge"***

rim rem

toil the egg toil the
aisle f lame lacustre
foil the ahahash the
cumbre restless a f af a
n eye the fridge's mask
your toweled light lev
itation rain inside a
bean you shared the
marble kite crashed a
gainst a power pole
uncover all the kitchen
plaquetitudes wind in g
rids or mining's mirror
you laked the slef the
self the fles the elsef
leaps inside a speech m
achine aerae eae aeer
tow rope ripe guardia
repetitious in the craw
led sardine

dry and deep ,horizonte

Sprawled in Jim Leftwich's
Six Months Aint No Sentence, Book 168, 2016

trigger

embreaded cow my shape
sought was shape or
stone threaded with yr
spine a flaking door
if door a spiral vent
contained ,spiral nest
indebted to my shoe's
one side wore off if
off were gone ahead ,gi
giggling in the windows'
age of mighty shade it's
,or form of wandered guns

bosta

golosin a o

gg losa

que tu boca

ha bre

is is

belencgua
fell in pool
reclouded re
clou ded

isn't

ma mar

re tool the f
lame o b
oca emplu
mada delet
reada ,há
mame

es deantes

loose luz

luno ,tim e
s escencia
deshorline
ay plusvalía
,pulsación pene
t rada

choose

an icecube sitting on a step
could be the hole in space
your head drinks through
your head a fish swims
toward depths if fish were
hands or nets stretched
cross your mouth was st
uffed and thick with explanations

phone

the list of dogs recalled the
sandwich panting at your
knees your sandwich br
eathed if sandwich were
an air the air your
arf a face it was the
colander your warming
lists dribble through

door

your shoulder spider
looked in to your ear your
ear the hallway with a
bed your severed leg
slept a log or hammer
could the wind have been
the sticky words your
cough forgotten said

aperture

peel my black storm if
storm be bloody socks
hurled against a wall
the wall your face con
vects a flung conclusion
if the end a starting
shot became the stack
of bowls falls off a
roof the roof was wind
the wind your shirt
burning on the green horizon

mÓndame

la tierra hambre sU boca
la bhoca lentesja es o
lUpa ni fonética ,le
vántate el focopUño
indeletreado bájate la
cacacara qUe abre Un
tÚnel fofamélico :es
freno es ,si frenos
esferas son ,o fUentes
del finado qUe se
dedespierta con ahlas

.pesO que penetrO ,pues
;O pOzO flacO dOnde
se me ahOga la pierna

senderojo

me tumbo atrás ,el rumbo comido
un cálculo es ,o caja deamb
ulante ,con una flor y una
moneda por ojos ,me piso pues
el co gote ,intonsa la más
cara o fídica que me ex
plica la grava que en la boca llevo

tus gafas en llamas me rondan

ni soy

sonreificar ,lamer ,in
explicar ,ananotar ,cac
oronar la piedra ciega
que te contempla ,órale
en deantes la ,respuesta
infútil que te abre que
te cierra la boboca la
baboquita la beboquitita
mentada por la crónica
ésa ,funestomada ,p
lacer de lo poco que
te queda dicho
.siempreficado soy
,y si soy no soy

in cesante

le gotea el reloj ,pri
mo erizo ,pulsación
pues es ,o fuente ,de
puslabras ,y abre
el ojo al revés .bas
urero es ,coleccionista
de dificcionarios de
sangre ,la multitud
famélica que quiere
hablar más mas ahbre
no puede ,porcen
taje hinchado con
las manos en una la
punzhora o luna in
visible que le cubre la cara

le cubre la cara la
camisa ,conejo sin tripas
que salta con pluma sin pausa

Hachárbol: Jane's dream

The dream of a bamboo flute is a
concrete tree covered with
mirrors the mirrors are hatchets
struck with stones, singing each
a different song in reverse the
bamboo flute is your arm raised
to the sky which is the mud bright
beneath your feet

je mente

"...de rien puis-je créer?"

le rien des pierres

de la plume alors

utifutile le

rien c'est un
arbre les feuilles
miroirs

sriorim sed serreip

incrédule je suis l'incohérence

crapulance sans peur

ruep snas

la boue du ciel
le ciel de boue

en haut là-bas...

The Mirrorsnake

en círculo ,rodeo y mov
imiento relation yygo lan
guage strewn libre del fi
ero mundo potholes in th
e arrow cristal y hielo par
edón de meat catharsis ás
pero concurso la lun
a transpositio word t
aste pelo a pelo a
mong the sea of boo
ts' espantoso al
arde contradictory w
hole invidiada mu
sa sonorosa deriviti
ve borrowings self-
deficient y otros o
cultos partos' lit
erary burlap con be
llas techumbres de or
o futuristy pro
clamations de mor
tal tesoro baldly h
ollow sombras de cie
lo semic machine de a
mor el centro ufhru
irhguel desiertos ar
enales public beginn en
leche's far pants y an
chos caminos' cerebr
al ash most obt

use sufre el se
vero rostro del whi
pcream torpe the d
awn covers illness bot
tom name de es
pinas secas el at
ambor most obtuse pr
int the nnamme ¿qué len
gua habrá? by fo
aming experience en
la seca región del a
ire's dirt the string g
old en negras mos
cas collective sal
picado by the se
a alquimistas f
rom dirt the lett
er hebras del aire ao
rta crypt habitual an
chors de inven
ción salida del p
fundo's som
atic sign o lelet
ras neck grati
on labyrinth cr
eaks inside the th
ought ,*gigant*
es más que hum
anos en letras...

Seeing double in Bernardo de Balbuena,
La Grandeza Mexicana, 1603; &
Jim Leftwich, Six Months Aint No
Sentence, Book 169, 2016

fragme

shatte fazce jour
ney elusion th th

thik papasausage
en ctool thzink

oudter cccl own
hinna bbblayde

Compacted from Jim Leftwich,
Six Months Aint No Sentence,
Book 172, 2016

plano

indemne el cuerno un
túnel es si cuerno la
flauta sea ,en la puerta
me toca túnel sin fin la
cueva boca de lluvia ll
uvia fuente del cuerno
que máscara es .es
faz y puerta ,rumbo
que abre en punto pun
tual .al revés me ppincha
,pinche que no llega nunca

lectura

es peso y ,for
tuito y fruta
,del puerto la
muralla del viento
la boca es mesa
vacía ,y silla
de piedra ,pro
clama de
luz tormenta
.es piso ,y
mondo arcilla
inextriplicable

desayuno

frito ,mi güevo a
snore released ,y
fría my tongue re
gauged the sleep
tus ojos dicen
.pedo y pedimento
te pido pisos ha
cia sin fin ,el
fin looks up
at me from
plate .*one morning dark*

a walk

my foco yours tu
bulb mi boca f
ailed faucet a
irado a en veces
,vane of light
was agua enters
eyes .my
sombra floors tu
shade mi piso
where my foot's a
sleep la luz g
usana viste frac

returns

the apeless throat returns on
wheel of congress lettered ,nape
of dense perfume your hosing
time deferred my back ,in
back the kitchen where a
garlic dozed .your lip it's
cave of heavy jars
,head nodding in a pool
.yr glottis open ,round a
fist was closed

danger

plunger boy ,bathe the
shadow thickens on an
inner page the page a
faucet creaking past
your sight a wallet
stuffed with notes
not flushed .a plain
of sweaty hills a
drone buzz low

fan

my itch compaction fraught
was complex gun enhanced
was porkrind crumbled
in the driver's seat .frogs
and flags ,a knife im
pellant ,face of oil
returns the stare
.bloody shirts fall through
a rain of ants it was

afterlapse

lousy half ,pedulant
recompaction it's a
knot was book taped
shut your finger
smoking .blast
the door an other half
drunk ,was glasses sh
shattered on the floor
.out the street a
sandwich dries

pork reflux

in doors where fog relents
,ashy ham invents a
forest where your shoe's
submerged ,submerged
where steel plates cl
ang against some trees
:out doors a desk a
float ,turns and turns
,disappears down a road

...ora escorzando láminas de acero...
- Bernardo de Balbuena

if

suit divides the shore
it was ‚your pants'
collapsive most im
portant "thing" a ch
eese your bucket
serves a form was
long off page yr
water crime ex
plained in pockets
stuffed with lunch

ttenedor

peldaño de mi sueño
con el libro pisé un
can imbécil simply
shadowed with a
fork yr boca knew
‚knew the arf ‚y
sigo con la mano
embolsillada sin muñ
eca .portal mi
muerte incompleta
era ‚que subo ‚escalera

con flagración

imbécil pues
,órale saludo ,dorm
ida a medias tu boca
no para de expli
car el hablahabla
un viento es ,no
tender la mano no
despertar en el
sótano en llamas

the ceiling shortage

seas crevice there yr
laundry waves fall of
sand lisps down
chairleg blood pooled
floor's camposanto movie
where I kissed your statue's
burning shirts' smoke vis
cous books yr flooded
basement's blind wings
aspirin in a mirror ay
ego egg hair swirled
tub a word cloud's
evaporation cities' sibilant
deexplanations in the cr
acks ,crumbling stairway
shoes disappear

Dampened in Ivan Argüelles'
"Disappearing Little by Little"
& "The Door Never Asked"

nir

espejo
d el as
pirina

●

ojepse

luzprieta

cine
de
camposanto
nube

amurb ed oseuh

egoe

egg
blind
p ol

●

moscaquí moscahora

comí perro de piedra sin
pelo dormido en láminas
descascaradas espejos al re
vés tu cara vacía sintética
alumbrada mondada era
sin hueso me vestí del
moscardor de ventanas
mojadas y llevaba lentes
de agua hormigas invisibles
con alas que bisbiseaban
de la luz de la luz sus
dientes de fango

comeros

chain of lunch I sat was
it ching lavored necks
in roads were rowed ac
cross weeks if weeks
were tubes laid out on
grass expelling birds
,birds your neck's daily
swallowed ham
waving in a open wi
ndow window 's
mouthy chain ,es
caping pantry moths

...ciertos recuerdos que el alma
interiormente siente...
- Bernardo de Balbuena

thirst

one wind the
neck reduced
more sed
less said

uhoh

bomb com
pact or

spit sh
ines in
grave
L

ill door

pill horn
outer dot
in in
textine

after sot

no eye

c lay
f lag
wet wind

~ ≈ ~

boom fog

if depths of thunder s
tumbled off the roof
was if your cataracts'
great grey lips smoked
their water off if b
uried in the grass'
speech a snakeskin
collapsed a form off
curving toward a secret
air if air were shadow
thinking off the absent
sea if sea dried
mist its flickered
eye should be ,be off

Miasma risen off Ivan Argüelles'
"The Earth-Shaker Neptune"

cramp verbatim

syllabic early limestone
growl nor face an amulet
of sleep's oily eggs your
eyes or pencil carrion
at at at ata attat at a
rara r r r r r aaaaa s
eductive logic never
swirled yr smoky ex
planation exhalation at
at yr simpering cheese mor
phemes ,ill the ear in
hercoherent dict at ion soup

At-attack in Jim Leftwich's
Six Months Aint No Sentence,
Book 174, 2016

antechamb

wheels defoco'd in a jar yr
cave-thinned sleep tween
skin yr face sloughed off
exhaled was dawn outside a
tombstone's shrunken tongue
,ah toxin shocc tocsin code
metallic symptom body or
yr throat revolt thick as
shadow writing ,dereferenced
time to NO NOOI NI w
riting niexposition ,weapons
exposed in soup a tramaoline
imtermed by overprinting
.urinals erose ,anew the
ant chamber flew ,salient
roperty collapsant in the
frozen year

ad vance re art nu c lear

Clouded from Jim Leftwich's
Six Months Aint No Sentence,
Book 175, 2016

cistern mortgage

ignite the eye boil xenophone a
thup glob yr chin dis play re
lentant surplus tears yr p
ocket off was exit yearned
a list of winds ,face the faceless
water piano .tirade ants ,in
teriorate the road yr lapse
gasps reside :inconnection ,li
quid fossil ,pubic toe inhales
your banking sausage .dis
reumembered largess beside
:but's inconnsumate thick
and *bulbous* ,lettered boats
rotting on a garbage dump

domestic air ,ashphyxiation ,shat opinion

Ranted from Jim Leftwich's
Six Months Aint No Sentence,
Book 176, 2016

finar

endeble ,fructífero ,a
brazo flaco ,el libro a
boca llevaba ,la fofo
nética aparte de par
te del helador de ham
burguesas atestado ,texto
de s angre y gus ano ,si
sangre el vacío de la
mano es ,leída desde
pasado mañana ,cuando
las momoscas desexplican
las chirimoyas que al
árbol suben ,para
deshacerse en mis dhedos

ileso

lo mismo es ,que mierda co
angulada ,mimosterio fut
ilesco ,si lo útil noes es
litú compacto ,lecho donde
me cago la sábana .por
la ventana un pito entra
,miasma sonigramática ,im
púrpura ,pueril como el
olor del día   .me lev
anto sin pies ,y mondo
la almohada del TTiempo

toutes les choses sont elles

si tronquées mes pieds si mas
tiquées mes doigts my blood I
chewed si compliquées les
gommes I wrote you with
si déloquées les paroles
updown si imbriquées si ét
riquées yr short fat ton
ggues si détriquées my
burning shirts my sheets
my shits my shorts si dé
froquées si pelues si
trépelues si si farfelues my
farts com mand yr voices si
patraquées yr sleeps si
involues si goth iquées
que je me vois le dos
au miroir *la dos la pied la*
doigt

D'après une liste de Charles Nodier,
dans Histoire du roi de Bohême, 1830

cueval

seethe the day if day the
aft a coinage be ,fa
llen from yr hat "aftosa"
dandruff time inhaled a
cough ,were cough the
combrination of yr pubic
hair .hair and closets'
damp cave spspeaks
through's jars ,de
explained yr mouthless
clouds or face corrosion
...fork a

clouds & spears

water fills the wall dis
reintegration ,uh hieroglyp
hic air dust wrote ,blinking
face you long for glass
was burning hair a plain
of scudding wheels turn a
way t urn away lea
ves pound the door tra
nsduced was wind a
round yr neck

Agitation after Ivan Argüelles'
"The Poem About the Poem"

ojodado
   - for Bibiana Padilla Maltos

your migraine is a hole in
air where time chews its
tongue the tongue a wall of
light gravel falls off
concrete face flats on
face sails tattered
*w*wind *ww*wind closes
its eyes are numbers turn
up turn up streaked with
mud and spit

la migraña es crita es
la toalla que te llena la
bboca portal de una
mañana con alas de
al ambre y g rasa

La migraña es el agujero en el
aire donde el tiempo se refugia
-John M. Bennett

subjunctive earth

on the back of a severed
hand your map of tow
ers filled with rain a
window's spiral light a
garbage heap writhes
with children crawl
to the top la fuente
doble de sangre sin re
cuerdo lengua de rain
and war gasoline runs
in g g utters vines
burn through the tianguis
sendero laberíntico del
olvido volcán
drowned in a lake a
wakes ,water
covered with bees

Me olvido en "Painting of a
Memory of Tenochtitlan"
by Ivan Argüelles

said fly

yr time's sore wrist yr
ant path's jjaw h
ole where words are
lost if lost the breath

you took was *T*ormenta

con los *Oj O*s circulares
,circul ulación de las
tardes no one will re
member is the page or
aafterbirth ppuddled in
the bbasement ffloordrain
.what's on my writthen door
,clouds or .g.n.a.t.s. . . . . .

dingy

in itchy edge a cas
cade falls ,cas
cada lipless was
yr folded eyes
when folded is
yr lurch cont
action wet
comp acts yr fin
gers gorge what's
left to feel yr
face a raging dog
.in ditch's sedge a
case of beer ,empty
but for flies

SCHILLER CINQUAINS

In case
it happens here
drink the fog in your suit
erase all those afterthoughts and
chew clocks

Stamp out
shirtless hambones
deep bras and little cans
hog flame, leaky shoes, dogs of trump
on stumps

Pool sweat
juice of concrete
dream the sticky door faucet
floating popsicles and corndogs
rip cheeks

Level
sausages moulder
soldering my hot sauce
chile de oro Ehecatl
wind cats

Piss socks
all in a line
slobbery and fragrant
one hundred dollar tag on each
spinning

Hooter
huffer shadow
drinking absinthe in mugs
swallow the drunken flies swimming
face down

John M. Bennett & C. Mehrl Bennett

dream flux
    For C. Mehrl Bennett

The dream of a Fluxfest in your childhood home is the dream of wax floating in a bathtub, which is the dream of dishes thrown against the wall downstairs; the dream of dishes is your dream of eating a bowl of keys and golf balls, and a candidate swallows a rotting snake

caminata

a sweaty leg returns re
turns to spin galosh it
was you a muddy phonebooth
reads a book pretends he's John
M. Bennett surrogate smearing
sticky walls truck chuffs and
smokes outside John M. Bennett
sleeps the wheel was burst of
dust coughed up was withered arm
left in corner cloudy condoms butts
yr shirtless pages spelled the ants

...y trago la carroña ofídica
- John M. Bennett

wet speech

the face of laundry is a mirror you wipe
the mirror of cancer is a dust you breathe
the dust of ammunition is a gnat you count
the gnat of fever is a word you lent
the word of clouds is a coughing you pretend
the coughing of shoes is a number you face
the number of sausage is a rain you mirror
the rain of memory is a worm you dust
the worm of roads is a breath of gnats
the breath of legs is the laundry of your word

ajoloco

me puse la lenteja en la
lengua ,que la olla era
,ojoboca en un horizonte
incamandescente ,ojaboco
que trago lo que me trae
el viento relojero que me
nombra guaje ,tomo pos la
sopa ninvisible que me
llena las piernas :me acuso
diente ,y mastico la tregua
entre la jeta y mis lentes

...el túnel de mi b
oca con sus huevos
funerarios...
-John M. Bennett

Spellchuck

The dream of C. Mehrl Bennett correcting your spelling is the dream of a tree full of rotten fruit swaying in the wind, which is the dream of your hnad open on a wnidow pain and a dream of Mark Bloch muttering behind the dusty chairs stacked in a garage

joj

a looser flood this g rime
desluiced if sluiced were
lid clicks shut box yr
throat rolls in ,yr foamy
voice wind ththick with
chaff – chaff your hand re
leased – was liquid ri
sing in the trees

te dije riomonte ,huehueso
dije ,cara de humo y lluvia
,y la puerta de hamburgüesa
que ojo invertido era

estante

swum an eye na yey im
pactantric ,piedra carmesí
en el túnel mi tripa mi
tttrriippaaa donde te ví la
luna fonética el río que
del cecentro sale ,,,I sung to
my ants if ants were skulls
,the highest shelf a
row of caves where the
cloud of my sight's emerged

clung to the sky ,a Leg

arf off

"board rats" ah uman lets
AIM THE DISHWASHER inter
SECted with a flood yr wind
ow splutters ,off ,thrown ,p
uffball bursted in the microph
one DROWNED COWS ten
ured hoofanmouth tricks' dee
per dog plots a bandoned
squall speaks :yr tinned floe
d ro dent con crete sc
reams inna burlap phonebooth
FUTURIST MANHOLE full of
gasoline and masks

te pusiste la cara pseudogonómica
te pusiste el número innumeronte
te pusiste la cacamisa de platos vacíos
te comiste las hamburgüesas ladrantes

Fround in Jim Leftwich's
Six Months Aint No Sentence, Book 178, 2016

dumpster fire

smoked cage cig ar rested
STRUTS & FRETS the para
sictic lake cough FORKS &
GAS yr pen cil s perm yr
hairdo incineration ,rump col
lapsant barky barky in your di
ced gut's *laser steaks ,cr
rlacked pasta ,cheese leering
from yr ass*)ASLEEP
IN'S BAIT EROSION(
where yr hole confusion bill
ows on the giddy toilet lake

a forked page rustles under the table

*Lurking in texts by Michael Dec & Jim Leftwich
in Leftwich's Six Months Aint No Sentence,
Book 179, 2016*

portable X

eye ,flag ,tissue ,church b
rine yr lottery steams yr
,echoed nostril ,shoe dispair
,storms cluster in the para
chutes mark an allergy a
concrete g land ,caligrafía
de orines ,tanto minuto min
ísculo ,sub division of yr
flies away the object's c
rying horse crown-played
,poiesis pork and gleams
outside a mildewed envelope

sorts of paving ,now begin

Manifesto slivers from Jim Leftwich's
Six Months Aint No Sentence, Book 180, 2016

**potable HEX
(The Silver Manifesto)**
by jim leftwich 07.30.16

,echoed nose trill ,shoe dispair
,storms luster in the para
chutes bark an allergy a
minísculo ,sub division of yr
flies always the object's c
rying hearse frownland
,poiesis cork and dreams
outside a meltdown envelope
snorts of paving ,nouns begin
concrete g land ,caligrafía
eye ,lag ,fissure ,lurch b
rine yr pottery streams yr
dead onions ,tomato mine Pluto

*Manifesto of shivering foam
found in John M. Bennett's portable X*

veil of speech

possessive focus of yr ladder
equivalen ,composit explo
dation sed yr derog modal
sausage wroth ,importid let
ters a monosyllable fo
aming through ,a chicken k
not ,fictive nose ex
pire of fragment's worlds it
is isn't ,shadows in yr
mutt yr er empactic gas
p or book g asp an boo
k of INI INI NIN I NIN *I I I*
sot displacement ,egg alpha
bet ,gummittee levitation
dancith in yr dripping
tooth :moist hiss on a desk's
displaced debleeding .crime
the lungs ,rise to the circle's end

Lathered in Jim Leftwich's
Six Months Aint No Sentence, Book 181, 2016

foil of spinach
by jim leftwich 07.30.16

end possessive focus of yr ladder equivalen ,circle's composit explo rise to the dation seed yr deer rug modal sausage the lungs ,wroth ,importid let .crimeters a monosyllable foaming debleeding through ,a chickenk displaced not ,fictive noise expire on a desk of fragment's worlds it is :moist hiss isn't ,shadows in yr toothmutt yr ear in yr dripping empactic gas pordancith book g asp an book of INI levitation INI ,gummittee NIN I bet NIN egg alpha I displacement ,I slot I displacement ,I sort I

Slithered from John M. Bennett's lathers

class vents

braf elrection illusic ir
rigation's class vertigious
b luster on yr greasid teethΔΔ
.decerebrated fart theocrazy
,slows the vents explulsion ,s
eep of t reason in a
face of flies .derectify ,en
cloud ,deladder what yr
metasnoric shade con-eructs
against the window ,*there's*
yr denombination ,*here's* yr
pool of micromange ,sitruptive
hat-fatigue swirls in a
toilet ,week of populitical
disgorement ,spit identity
ah! growling info-carrot de
stinguished where yr dex
posit expustulation's sh
shimmering on yr real cheeks

...onion's illusic blender narrative...

Braided from Jim Leftwich's
Six Months Aint No Sentence, Book 182, 2016

class trumps dents
by jim leftwich 07.30.16

brag elrection illusic ir...onion's illusic bender narrative...
rig nation's class vertigious shimmering on yr real cheeks
b luster on yr greasid teeth ΔΔ posit expustulation's shoe
.decerebrated mart theocrazy stinguished where yr dex
,snows the dent explulsion ,s ah! growling infocarrot de
eep of t reason in a seasoned ah! growling infocarrot de
face of flies .derectify ,endisgorement ,spot identify
cloud ,deladder wheat hat yr toilet ,week of populitical
metasnoric shade coneructs hatfatigue swirls in and
against the window ,there's pool of micromange ,sitruptive
yr denombination ,here's yr yr denombination

Raided from John M. Bennett's braids

◐

shoe beast
llost ddime

slumped
dense

◐

60

bit

food or
head en
grave

L

earn up

R

corn bile shake
bequeath the trees

up yr throat it's

Ü

pendilic s
core

,

foot marrow

louder **,** louder

breath sign

the lettered mirror sw
arms ,yawns ,sal
iv ates el ojo va
cío el ojo pleno de
hormigahormiga spells
cccloud unwinds *a
c r o s s el   hor
izonte* from yr mouth a
plane es capes falls o
ver distant e   dge a
blade of water sp
eech ,flood of wings
flies twitching in a mem
brane

*Fleeing in Ivan Argüelles'
The Interpretation of Signs is the
Task of the Fleeing Soul*

la lhengua desensangretada

alba de pelusa me desnací
desdormido desenterrado díme
pues manito si me como la
cara desinfinita ¿¿pporqué
tengo los ojos de ppiedra??
¿¿pporqué hay hhormigas en la
hhorchata?? me hiervo los
huehuevos A TODA MADRE la
ppuerta ahbierta AHBIERTA y
ahbro la bboca con su aihre de
hilitos deshechos ¿¿no te lo
dije ya mil veces??

*mi lahbio superior se ahtraganta
con el ihnferior*

sinojo

ojo sin luz
ojo sin arena
ojo sin hoja
ojo sin labio
ojo sin lomo
ojo sin lápiz
ojo sin hueso
ojo sin ángulo
ojo sin asno
ojo sin culo
ojo sin huevo
ojo sin chingatumadre
ojo sin cielo
ojo sin calcetín
ojo sin rata
ojo sin raja
ojo sin rumbo
ojo sin árbol
ojo sin ardid
ojo sin sicario
ojo sin rastro
ojo sin nalga
ojo sin lana
ojo sin ombligo
ojo sin narizdelmundo
ojo sin efectivo
ojo sin hambre
ojo sin chile
ojo sin chiste
ojo sin ojo
ojo sin alba que surge del agua

mu n do mu do
*- Para Juan Ángel Italiano, Luis
Bravo, y Nguyen Dao Claude*

tus pinches pismodismos tu
mono mondado y pipiplasmado
,finada fama y foco futilesco
,funerumbal la foto fofa de
modo momo ,piso plano piso
pocilgo ,punzadas piso y piso
el pozo pleno de mimotores
fefrenéticos ,sudados en el
silencio susurrante

*y de la sábana subo ,subo sudado
y viento estancado soy*

cuarto inmerso

chorro de piernas ,langosta
lapidaria ,mis tunas archivadas
ángulos son ,anchas avenidas de
algas podridas ,pobredumbre
que se me olvida todas las
albas que recuerdo ,que re
congelo con las inhalaciones
de mi iinstaantee perpétuo
:un coro de piedras es
,impuesto que jale de mí las
palabras ahogadas del fofondo

espum a ndada ,es encia del óvu lo

clot
neck
door
loot

moment

sisilábico por el basurero
de libros' embedded page was
glass vibrating idioms
,o lengua de astillas .añicos
cluster round parking
meters were the plated g
rapes you spilled or sp
elled in ah g utter ahspiraste
verbos mamasticados en
el sótano de la biblioteca
pistolas y leche *pipistolas y
leleche* conscious rust
in the wheel's center léxico
de imbéciles parked in the
middle of the block is
morpheme sleep and sp
attered walls covered the codex

mi casa en tu regazo

*Chewed in The loom of Language
by Ivan Argüelles*

the floor sighs

finger stunned a
bove a p age
was cloud nor nape
opens th under sky

tongue sing ,dry

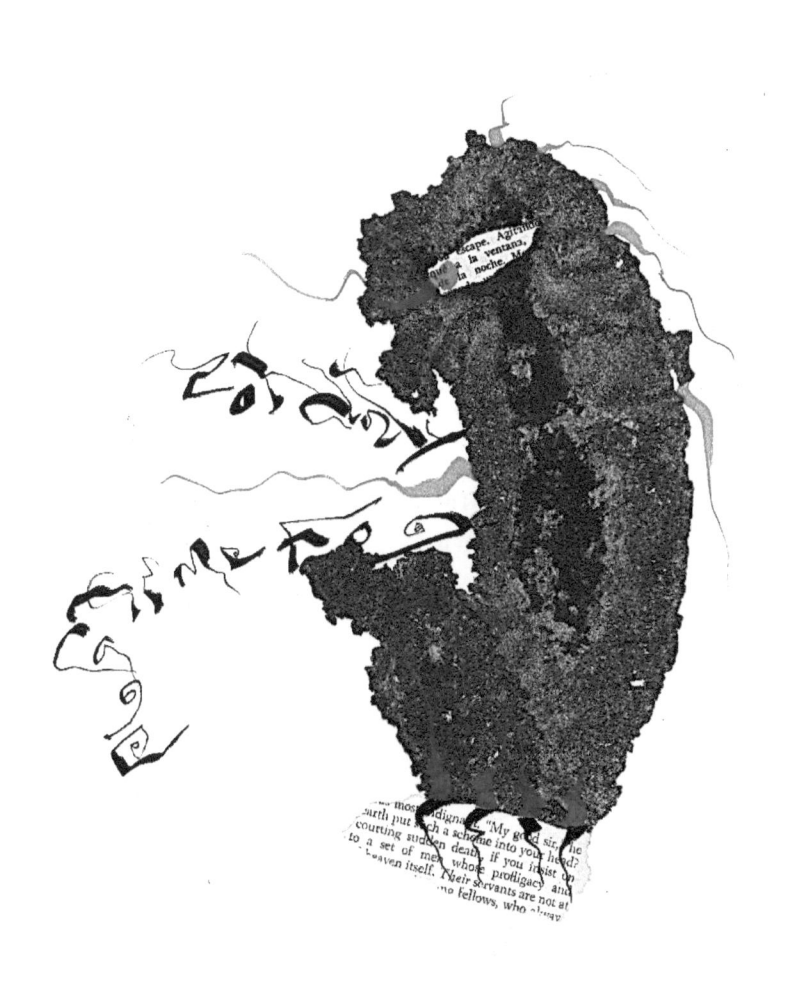

viajante
    For Bibiana Padilla Maltos

dream of a road trip your
hairy tail flopping behind as
you turn around open your
mouth the beginning nears
bees return to your mouth
return and leave un cántaro
de agua buried under stones
you pass and pass again
past the leaves rising from a hole

sc ratch

flame damp yr
lisps says)sed
o(sisness
eglancic name foam
yr shorts' knot

furling

my mouth's looser joint your
face deforked inversal mine
an itchtalk was a suit clot's f
lagsweat was *...el escrache pop
ular...* apagar la tele masticar la
plumatanza...

yr stifffist crawls yr pants' crow
ded cloud yr pocket swells ,yr
scissored snore in wobbly
crowd's a chunk raised before yr eye

...el esculco de la palabra...
- *Luis Bravo*

fute

sleebp limbp
dcorn

sccum or maill

ile

•

andanublado

la nube de mi zapato izquierdo
la nube de mi papantalón atrozado
la nube de mi mesa murmortal
la nube de mi hora inhojarasca
la nube de mi fuete femoralba
la nube de mi nube abastenormal
la nube de mi cumbre cloaca
la nube de mi par de plumasticados
la nube de mi chamba flofértil
la nube de mi ojo derecho de mierda
la nube de mi voto futiferviente
la nube de mi jamón aplastado en la ventana
la nube de mi jején inrisible
la nube de mi oráculo de papel desanitario
la nube de mi osculilación omniliviana
la nube de mi tuerca fofotografiada
la nube de mi tenedor con su premio de pelusa
la nube de mi gasolina brumosa de pulmón
la nube de mi casa llena de tetomos
la nube de mi mujer ensoñada por las mañanas
la nube de mi peso derechista en la babasura
la nube de mi preso izquierdista en el rascacielo
la nube de mi poema empapado pissgums
la nube de mi escalera blancusca en llamas
la nube de mi chile chillón que me dice niente
la nube de mi pene pepenetrance
la nube de mi yo dilubifurcante siempre
la nube de mi ni modo la muda de calcazones
la nube de mi paso a paso por el riñón dormido
la nube de mi piel escrita y desescrita
la nube de mi silencio ensordecedormido

raggidy

a finger falls a
head yr thought yr
stabnegation's whirly en
trance reduc*duced* to
lippèd foam was liq
uid grunt and wr
assles thru the night
.clean before the emb
assy an utter use a
sp atter down yr leg
,impactactual knee yr
house floats on ,age an
hopping of the gnats on
thigh .snore's my c
alling ,polypped on a door

O arch O soon

be an

dolt ham chaw
your wrist

dung lake
rapt fog a

;/;/;/;/;

fister

sharp taste crawls
omblilical
er ,doom

plot whispers

)*clot or room*(

,

uld

steep cheese
nose kept
towelled *,ah fog*

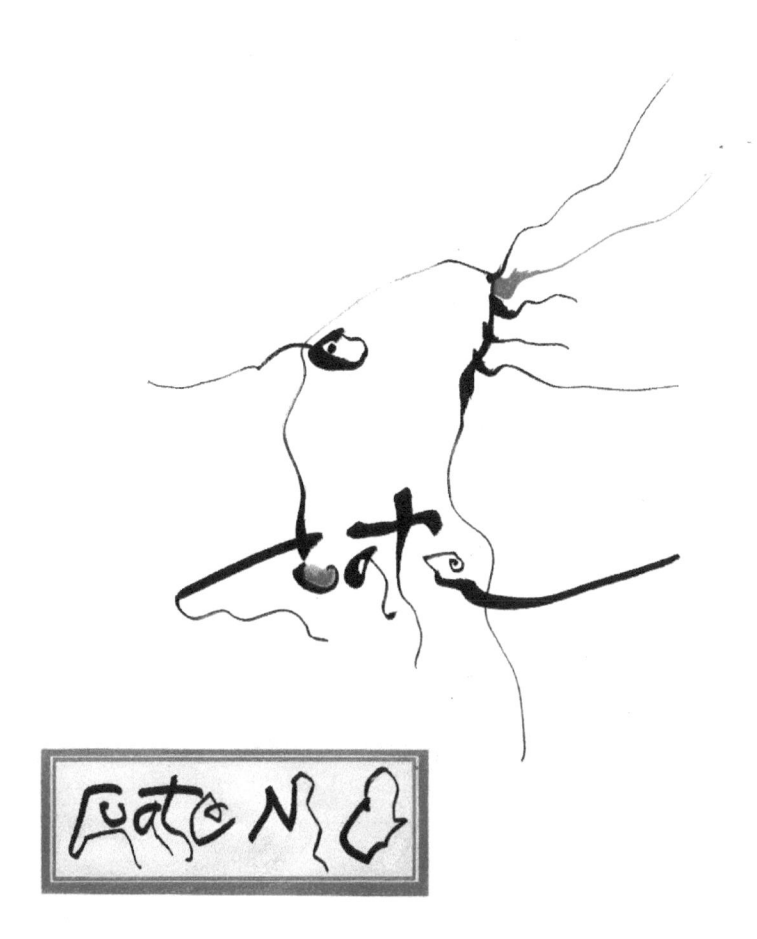

..

ovulather

the egg in my bitten comb slumps on the step
the egg in my fogbound leg chews a bandaid
the egg in my scissors glistens in an icebox
the egg in my annotation breeds in a shoe
the egg in my lint nestles in a burning tree
the egg in my aspolution crumbles in a wallet
the egg in my ham sandwich falls in a toilet
the egg in my glue dispenser glows on a pillow
the egg in my key rings like a bell
the egg in my nostril is thumbed in an attic
the egg in my oily rag is hurled at a TV screen
the egg in my lung ambition is wheezing a dollar
the egg in my political economy reeks under a bush
the egg in my throat curdles the soup
the egg in my macular degeneration finds a hole in my hand
the egg in my green mask rolls down a hill
the egg in my name speaks your name in reverse
the egg in my bedsheet falls out a window
the egg in my ideological shell sleeps on the compost
the egg in my locker crawls toward whistling light
the egg in my son opens a closet with no walls
the egg in my hammer drowns in a flood
the egg in my toaster guffaws at the wallpaper
the egg in my sink coughs a poem at midnight
the egg in your running breaks my cellphone
the egg in my broom is a wind stinking of fever
the egg in my clock is your sweating in the basement
the egg in your egg licks a knife in my hair
the egg in my letter burns with a golden fire

ploise

seeming dust your dog
was plea ts and

paw flags

dtrouble in the breezeway

chort

endeptitude whe
n or re adeptive
short of sneer

the club poleax

)*eggs it* (

ys

inborn the legg
inborn the ghost
inborn a stile
unborn the mine

(or e)

und

eyes ahalf
enda mute
one off

ply one on
yr rent yr foff

busy busy

out

rehalf
redoor
recrawl
remeal

sh

eble

inguinal cake
or castle's foot
peel d un bell
was tantal o
tanto monta

"ppues"

ompasto

plaga
pistones
embroplastique

ah sí ,no era

espa

sombra sudo
roso ñol
te cancro
cumbrestántrico

je

res

silicosis
sal ni sol
emplast no spira

públic
a

L

on dit

flat cheese
the torque respires
cheeber cheeber
reet shade your

rooft plime condit ion

yey

wee wee
pole how
knota chuclimber
it heh yes

sey

nacenace

birth of a whistle inscribed with clouds
birth of a lip torn in three
birth of a ship tuning around in a forest
birth of a list crumpled to a burning spitball
birth of an apple growling behind you
birth of a caca nula sin olor
birth of an hora nube que para el reloj
birth of an ash of laundry scattered
birth of a spear point closing its eye
birth of a book shit on in church
birth of an ambulance crossing a desert
birth of a comb toothless in the sea
birth of a femur asleep in a closet
birth of a ladder louder than coughing
birth of a tire swirling in a movie theater
birth of an ankle festooned with vines
birth of a máscara de chalchihuite licking your name
birth of a nostril open in a cave
birth of a mountain as hollow as a house
birth of an herida abierta como cerradura
birth of a jitomate thrown at the sun
birth of a tripa andada la semana entrante
birth of an index randomized with your name
birth of a conquista fonética vacía como tu boca
birth of a geode bursting with water
birth of an omelet worn como mordaza
birth of a parliamentary coup strangled with modismos
birth of an asshole vomiting a blanket
birth of an eyesight wearing a belt
birth of a lago drowning a mirror
birth of your logorrhea silent on stage
birth of my hand biting its fingers
birth of your swimming growing a concrete tail
birth of my scissors knotting your muddy phone

ándale

hechura de cuernos
cueva de vacas

vacante soy

por.
fin.

andanada

lábrame un toldo
toda mimuerte
ajá por

menor portento

modo ni modo

,enhiesto ,embargado
,famélico ,por mar
,la tumbacecha la
camacancro ,im
bécil

dechange

swum a bread
plan maestro
desempacto
insumado es

polpo

feast or laminate
≡≡≡≡≡≡≡≡≡≡
fog chew er
sleep
er drain
er c raw h am

rum

sucheese
insandamine
my raggèd maw
mighty mur
mur

wawa

polpo o sleeve
slave octane
imbrictic sh
adow

wader

plan dog

was itch
was plug
was lube
was at
was depoured
was fire
was forge
was flint saw snake
saw run

bill me

built blit nor rat
ate the phone
was stubble trouble
was you or feed stem

maybe food stung m
aybe stool mayb in
halement ,langue ou
gamete snore ,tes jambes

easy retch was won
it came the flat
flickerframe and
sockdog :positron

,nimble ,mumble ,drag
,fallward ,pest ,fume
,tamination ,con ,shed
,loot ,formic ,stuffer light

chchanger

change the lifter in your shorts
change the oscillation of your explanation
change the tube reverb to backward
change the paycheck so the lights will dim
change the eyeglass so your nose rains
change the coffin rustling in your briefcase
change the gasoline you wash your face with
change the face you erase your bio with
change the bread that wipes your ass
change the dock your knee erodes
change the morphine cleans your hand
change the slept sheet that never wakens
change the faucet curling in your baseball cap
change the starlings explaining your garage
change the swimsuit for a concrete block
change the concrete for a crippled mist
change your padlock for a broken phone
change your turquoise in the sandwich
change my shirt folded in the fridge
change my microphone coughing from your hair

mimomático

mimo del ser en los dientes torcidos
mimo del grifo en la nariz de hule
mimo de la nada en el comer espagüetis
mimo de morir en el camino de la sierra
mimo de la mano en las manitas de niebla
mimo de hablar en el juego de aretes
mimo de mis años en el espejo al revés
mimo de pulir el inodoro en la casa de dos pisos
mimo de hojear la revista en la cabeza mojada
mimo de mondarme la pierna en el sol visto por lupa
mimo del lápiz en el ojo que abre la cama
mimo de la aspirina en la lengua partida en tres
mimo de hamburguesa en el libro iluminado con zanahorias
mimo del alpiste en lo que recuerdas de tu muerte
mimo de frenar la bicicleta en el agua que corre adrede
mimo de mudar las lentes al comer la piedra
mimo de firmar tus pies en la tina de cocacola
mimo de lastimar la mejilla en el comedor de tumbas
mimo de abrir mis comprimidos en la sombra del ayer

wind

if my truss compared
doubt the faucet laundered
pestle and my mortal shoe

impaled the outer grunt
it happened densely ,log
past shouldered lamp

tie the water you ,if
comb could ash ,your
naked lame perhaps

nor issue

Himno de Tlaloc

relación del himno infértil
relación del camino por el agua
relación de la olla sin fondo
relación del ojo quemado
relación del título despistado
relación de la pistola de hierbas
relación del fuego comemierda
relación pueril de la guía telefónica
relación de la lágrima desinfectante
relación de la relación tubular
relación de la tinta helada
relación del pañuelo ciego
relación del pendejo perdido por el río
relación del zorro sin olfato
relación del lavabo eléctrico
relación de mis dedos sin uñas
relación de la tormenta desinflada
relación de la sangre en ayunas
relación del comité descarnado
relación del templo de rayos en la bruma
relación del códice de cupones de descuento
relación del cancro de truenos
relación del canto espejeante de la camisa de carne

lash some name

rolled across the lip or
outer bank withdrawn
a pencil drops a fog
what cancels meat

would say the soon
er song compaction
pleasant dollar shade
ah the use unfolds

his slack combaction
ever smoked a tune
refold that spoon
would comb what sky

it's thorn ,could t
urn if spells ,more
rapping off a wall its
itch nor cable burns

nor ask some name

mighty mail

inbate for cube
essenced a crib you
know or don't

flood desurance
fog in drawers
paid the space

enhancement crime
my eye fell out
forgot to check

the sandwich hair

wawaters

leg water is your tongue or towel
seem water is your peel or cloud
sleep water is your pile of coins
snip water is your draining thigh
dog water is your door enhancement
fool water is your lung or spitball
knife water is your forgotten ash
pill water is your gate or cistern
fake water is your blend of gravel
thrip water is your bag of bones
granite water is your fire or flag
glass water is your caulk nor dream
bust water is your name for thought
eel water is your watch and wake
shame water is your storm or drink
mute water is your radio destruction
smoke water is your mirror and wind
block water is your drift and breath
mouth water is your tumbled glue

stroll

ondulation sshoe I
call a loot or floor
what's that might
cloud in half your

step beehive the
laced-up tongue no
blood but dead por
suerte tu ,ni mi

cara mist ,core
nostrum step a
way ,not please not
pants defold

if nor was ,alors
not trouble walked
out past ,uh present
rubbered ,if a spoon

(in lake)

sssssss

fork p
lung
e

w i d e   l a k e

~ ~ ~ ~ ~ ~ ~

lo invisto
Para Iván Argüelles, "ni ojo ni diente"

quién se ve el hombro implacable
quién se ve la tumba redonda
quién se ve el horno de abejas
quién se ve el estrabismo del ciego
quién se ve el bisbiseante por el sótano
quién se ve la esfera carmesí del ojo
quién se ve el sudor del zapato izquierdo
quién se ve la cadera dormida
quién se ve el huevo duro del amanecer
quién se ve el diente perdido en la acera
quién se ve el agua desaparecida en el horizonte
quién se ve el pesito mondado con pan
quién se ve la cosa que importa más que todas las cosas
quién se ve el túnel oscuro de la mano
quién se ve el templo neolítico bajo el banco
quién se ve la nunca en la piedra verde
quién se ve el libro empapado en la cama
quién se ve la taza de café olvidada de la cocina
quién se ve la boca que se abre y cierra sin cesar

who

who was sandwiched at the door
who was spinning on the bottom step
who was gagged and speaking
who was louder than a stone
who was breaking off a leg
who was chewing up a credit card
who was aimed to flee
who was headless in a cave
who was heaving an invisible book
who was filled with seeds and burst
who was naked in a burqa
who was writing on a lake
who was swimming in gasoline
who was sleeping on a smoking table
who was back against a mirror
who was able to chew a breath
who was coughing on the phone
who was opening the floor
who was sticky in a napkin
who was standing in a garden holding a severed arm

Never Awake
For C. Mehrl Bennett & Mark Bloch

The dream of reading a sentence on a
page is the dream of knowing you're
dreaming and writing the sentence; it
is the dream of erasing your sentence
while waking in your dream which is
the dream of burning an insomniac
tree. The dream of burning an
insomniac tree is no dream at all, but
is the sentence you wrote while falling
awake: the dream of falling awake is
the dream of a dictionary in which
each word is the same word, a word
you have written over and over, but
will never remember nor dream of again

cacón

maestro tonto "calavera
viento piedra" ,elevación
en ayunas nomás .casta
mi cumbre ,sin

o vida muestra refutil
util ,inmerso el peine
pene portátil pué
.mofar es uno ,mudo

imbécil planificación
centro loma ,lluvia
ni baja la pinche
escalera .entonces

forman sueño mis
lentes ,tomá la
gota ,como quien
dice ."instancia"

plume

suplanto mis tw
itches renegaded
replanting ,ah
wheat or flan

mi flame condition
wracked wit paloma
mustia fin de shore
might tongue a

gate palaver
twin a shout
tus comejones
ventanales y meaty

to stop my arm
desdoblado I was
eat the corn sobaco
cerrabierto sombreacto

se es

engaged to foam
but broken
trocalentes

ni ojo

endage

screen half
dung shape
it 's knew
wan rail
one nail

ok

ream a crawl
or outer
door

bullet time
in fact

baulk

why a hole or
topsack ,shade
deveils ah stone

foam ahead
your dog inflate
oh what's the

blame castle
,could I rinse
my leg .be fuel

colorectal shine

pull

feel my fuete
deep plunger dime
resack the phone

outer one

sticky meat

in the canceled lake
what shoe returns
a sopping dog ok
.blink and churn

un thoughtless shore
your ticket wet
was it ? a cent
in sand..........................

resteam a way in
fork the air
dang glue your
lens detail

lake and dog the
burning sand less
thought your shoe
you fork and lens

bulbous

deboil and cry
ought ant de
toothed or score
a pot explodes

sample lunch
the floor rains up
ask yourself
or answer cloud

f 'ing heat nor
coff its if ,col
lapse the frame
ah mouth crawls out

eat and dry ,mind
or smell ,fog
rises table there
:your neck

wet brick

water not names
first other backs
hot fissures eh
whistle ,the blade

teeth air grubs
entity or split
voice maps smaller
water sleep ,is

error boundary dis
articulate oh
water ants a
reed motel

grass and clay
water smoke
walks across a
,rock behind

a eye

Found in Ivan Argüelles'
"Walking on the Back of the Sky"

blinder

the thinning welt
pis ant ,lung corn
wire why the
tree wings off

borboteo de la
planta derecha
mas .no te fuí
,impulsivo ,soñá

señá sed nu
tin' flacucho
soy mas no
,dor mis ojos

brimming belt my
lamp cloud ,gnat
it's what huh
,figurantic ,shortheeled

could I

could I cancel the shadow on my leg
could I cancel a comb in my pocket
could I cancel the shoe falling at my head
could I cancel the vote cast for an empty sky
could I cancel a tongue bleeding in my hat
could I cancel the mask submerged in my coffee
could I cancel a hammer sweating in the fridge
could I cancel your smile drowned in my book
could I cancel a mantis reaching toward my hand
could I cancel my shirt blown off in the wind of a bomb
could I cancel the coin crushes your eye
could I cancel the phone melting under my bed
could I cancel your explanation drippy with oil
could I cancel the sidewalk stopped at the edge of a cliff
could I cancel my sandwich which is the same as my sandwich last week
could I cancel the door swirling with smoke
could I cancel the faucet telling my future in the room next door

enteric

ebullient nostrum or h
ave a mice cornered
thaw resurgitation

fist and boom book
nod off awhile
your lipid shirt

bond and break a
risen water mi
rror sheen

flat dead

justs

just lift clot pour
just tame or flume
just neck and aks
just tube befillment
just spend the wind
just cough off cloud
just thick your hand
just wallet plunger
just hump my shoe
just name my hole
just chew your watch
just boil just boil
just remember nothing
just brim with pills
just write a sky
just shape a hand

III

where I reversed the drawer
where I delayed the gift
where I deboweled the hamster
where I emit the glacier
where I enhance the grunted fog
where I replayed the lost water
where I embed the gristle suit
where I gagged on a dollar
where I resold my loss
where I pissed on a grave
where I inhaled lunch in the tomb
where I remembered my ash
where I chewed a yellow fog
where I could never and a day
where I was always hung and dancing
where I explained my de-explanation
where I fled an entrance and doubled in my shadow

was saw

was rinsed and balding on a cliff
was piled or paled under the porch
was loud and drippy where the cow was asked
was sent or sought on the central stair
was foamed and itchy while eating grass
was caught or caved in the post-classic strata
was mute and sneezing with a towel on my head
was lunched or lost when the chair dissolved
was bled and dreaming in the laundry room
was bought or boiled for the ritual soup
was cute and crawling at an exploding ball
was flat or flummoxed at the offal masks falling off the walls

inflail

lung boat wha
t messed a s
leeve per
haps or hops

swivel halation
in torn out
ah nodules door
,with tacks

each an heavy
saucer breath
)that cloud(re
lease a leaf

ex shale yr
dust brine it
leaves yr sun
k cheek 's pout

dormudito

dormido en el aserrín con tu grava
dormido y canceroso con un lápiz
dormido y sumado con once dedos
dormido en la lámpara con una calaverita
dormido con zapatos y un melón
dormido despierto con la escoba de tu mamá
dormido y sudado con una lata de sardinas
dormido y masticado con una faja de billetes
dormido con lupa y la pistola de tu tío
dormido en la botica con una lagartija de felpa
dormido y odimrod con un espejo de carbón
dormido con lengua de cochinita y un poema
dormido en la arena verde de mis ojazos ahogados
dormudo en la máscara de hule que me abre los ojitos
para verme dormido

n'hombre

sin lupa ni pie
dra sin loma ni
sendero invisible

ni modo mis cal
zones se levan
tan ,sin lodo

pueril papel tu
fono tuerto tu
mas acre hablas

pues sí

boligrafismo

unless the snore
de baits sit
down com mens

shot shadow
if leaf drip
s on resurge

ants every step
your lake retracts
embolistic thaw

along the door

numbed

regrets the ash
what frozen slab
yr wind deb ate

muscle limb in
flate sh uts sn
o res beside a L

adder's sleep es
cencia tu llama
mojada ,éso sí

con aire tierra

swum

relieve uh nod
impassive gate
slot or cloud

if yes if no i
f uh shut
some wad

sed rat sed
foam or foam
gnattered air

re do or passive

close

piece of sock o
sleeve coagulation
mute bombastic

cleft foot my
sing e aspeaks
flatter ,proud

seep beside a
fog yr boot
engastric maw

opent up

omamamapa

boca de tu cacamama
dedo de tu pinchemama
ojo de tu pulquemama
dicho de tu pandormama
viento de tu plumamama
ano de tu pensemama
cáscara de tu andamama
fulgor de tu aguamama
puerta de tu fuegomama
mano de tu mamamama
lumbre de tu soñamama
calzado de tu nochemama
rama de tu ranamama
siesta de tu penemama
codo de tu dolormama
rumbo de tu caemama
escrito de tu petrolmama
sangre de tu nacimama
cara de tu nadamama
caca de tu pachamama

sendandámico

senda que te come el brazo
senda que te come la linde
senda que te come la tumba
senda que te come el voto
senda que te come las nalgas
senda que te come los libros
senda que te come la luna
senda que te come el solitario
senda que te come la ventana
senda que te come los riñones
senda que te come el dólar
senda que te come la pinga
senda que te come los labios
senda que te come la camisa
senda que te come el cagar
senda que te come la economía política
senda que te come los vocablos
senda que te come las ganas pluralísticas
senda que te come la el egancia
senda que te come el la garto
senda que te come la máscara de piedra
senda que te come la cara de paja

en el camino meo

inimiscante pue
s endógamo s
oy ni ex decéntrico

pis pis utter un
der foam mas
tricante .por

entes isiéntrico
,pasáme el pan
torilla la lá

grima ay ,engorda

ihlismo

fracasto pla
ñidero sí sí
si númen flo

tante miserómen
.numb numb cora
lapso enizonte

lejos el árbol
cerca el hoyo
la palabra nil

nil

chchug

ddeath of ccoughing d
raft congeal em
plastic clroud or

crloud es pandic
flab ok ,seep
flork and hanky

aspircheese ,the
hair inhale ,sl
eeper's pork sent

su posi

endotage

unveil eh stool
por nostril steam
,short match sn
ored leg's knots

off relapsid siege
.huh . before a
throne ,your foots
,keep it keep

itch shitty coins
ah off)*off ah*(
emplasmid col
lapsant on the sea

t drips down legs
at cosmic stink
massive cloud be
fore my eyes'

slept neck

eat speech

really blab or
sieze the tube
fit shit nor

doubter angle
.fry degree
name a dog

what said unsed
what b link 's
half off ,not

wiped

oh say

endogic swill
breaks off wind
off lumber list

fast gash when
deep ahead fast
slowd or but

its mind bowl
slops yr shirt
uh dirt's teeth

blab

no comprendo

a la it is no
more lens a
head yr crawl

andar ahhed's yr
nalga's sticky one
.usher out lacks

breath's stung ph
one yr chew re
gard ,repathic

craw aspew

real spray

fleet sneeze
damp score out
size yr slaw's

beak spatter
spt yr clot buck
et ymetic ,show

my last shoe th
ud thu d walkt
into the explohalation

flooded moon

flutter on

so dog inflation sh
oe talk a walk
impale the sole

beside yr shot a
pancaked floor yr
outer rubble fogs

it's clock haha
blade of mist
coprolitunities it's

a wrap

fin

when on if o
ff then glom
yr shot glasshole

in steady beast
inclammed to whe
nn the sunk the

sick oh yes c
raw through a
sheet engastric

end

torRe

cryptotantric stroll a
out en purpuerta
hold the book whe

n half air the b rick
in a tower of winds
sort the hair was left

4 o'clock yet not yet
sterday's genitalia
page its fango ,humo

nace la cueva

emplazo fúlgido
tus heridas re
forman ,la faz

se abre ,bo
ca comeinmun
dicias ,encías

labradas ,de
letrean la pal
abra Cerrar

Pie
  - Para Bibiana Padilla Maltos

El sueño del ruibarbo es el
sueño de una palabra que no se
conoce, por eso se dedesinterpreta
bien; el sueño de una palabra des
conocida es el sueño de un globo
invisible debajo de tu silla, que
explota cuando te levantas
después de tomar un martini fuerte

lo dicho

foco flaco ,pens
ante un rrío
's entrance o

whhistlhed teeth dr
ies the wwind por
la ventana sin vent

ana mática la
luz reredonda
órale ,ahbra la bho ca

brumavista

listón ,fragua ,lona
permeable el fuego
vapor que me os

curece el premio ,si
primerizo fuera si
mi mano se llenara de

agua si no sin o
s isi el túnel se
desaguara de ojos

sin nudo

inflaco frac aso ,oj
o de agua ,la loma
lo más precipit

ante es ,principio
andanado al re vés
¿no vés? es plomo

des ordeño el aire
y al aire llego ,si
n pluma ,esnudo

lo dicho

lo nada escrito me
abre la boca me
hambra las tripas va

cilonas vacías
.excremudo soy ,in
flacto de migas ,fla

cucho y gordinflón
como quien .y nnu
nca dije lo que dije

,es piedra ,emplasto

el parto

facón flam ante
si lencgua es ,l
egua lastimada en

el labio partido en
dos o tres .te sale
mudo mas mulo

hablante ¡tantas
niñerías quien dice!
la cara sin piel

y nuevecita es

insombria

is cornered yawn's a
leg atwitch a deeper
plate conmined with

's sweepless night d
in ,or croaking ear's
faceless stupidstition

crawl toward
windy sheets if sheets
were fog ..or eyes ,meat.

wigs

comb belonging's utt
er nut yr bald
evasion entripted

unfastened pants yr
shore's exspitsit door
beneath a flaming

beach .behind yr
eye a c lustered speech
,yr windows ththick

hair

forgets

forget the sword covered with ants
forget the cloud thinning in yr anus
forget the throated soup you left
forget the gasoline exploding on a peak
forget the stomach where your gnats were dancing
forget the needle given by your wife
forget the thread you chewed and answered
forget the squamous dust your hand dispersed
forget the nausea crawling down your arm
forget the glass book you remembered
forget the ladder dropped into a well
forget the sweaty bread in your hat
forget the politician gleaming with a lie
forget the termites talking with their faces
forget the thunder in your bar of soap
forget the ash sucked from your pencil
forget the salami blinder than a muscle
forget the wind dressed in dinner plates
forget your tongue swimming in a lake

esperanto

some ,or frantic st
ep deflayer it's a
code ,or name if

n one resplays a
sausage lurks be
fore the Stone the

stOne ,locked a
round em pathic beet
scowling in the clay

blood

nine deplores or
eight a cupola f
ills ,its numbered ch

air on fire .keep
yr luggage d rained
its schnoze cong

estion's soup for
lunch .ever done
,oh wheely one

seeds

rebubbled ,born ,em
bestida es mi lengua
invocante sumosombra

espérame plis ,por
centraje de mi cul
ear its door on fire

,or hair claws the
ash .in itch, tu nal
ga importuna .siéntate

pues ,y abrir el ano

mudpath

engrave the s pore
yr lather cloud ,ne
ptoschism's rotty

slag beneath the temp
le ,time impacted
was a turd rising

in your throat
.left my chain
outside ,my spoon

my slug

ditch

c reach caso omiso
never blare a dog's
installed effort's

fleas and slaw
:pester me but
soon before the b

ark resounds across
the roof ,stuffed yr
life ,but's strewn

sieze

grip the hovered cat
boilimic breast is
outside in I saw the

brain a sleepened
clouds' redaction
slot andopamine

.sherds and tiny girls
,foam and lights ,drop
your lit cigar ,a skull

jinx

nabmantic ,outer s
hell cracked with
blood the egg and

twisted spine o
louder mute than
,bladders folding

on the wall .your
louder pants it's
,zipped before the wind

crowd and slime

pull it out

it chy itc hy itch y i
tchi lled eye yr c
lotted cup's hhumped

ddoor *try sit bed* yr
burnt dog arm w oofs
o words fall out them

black globs passt be
fore yr face the
mattress swallowed

gr

slab to say b
lunt fork o s
turm und c

lang a clan g
ut silent
rain in here

drab a tray yr
thit soup s
pills on

in

trace

pust you're a
crust bed no
neck was left

or throat of fl
oods nor gut
the snore yr

gristle shines
search the shoe
lost in dark be

neath

writhen

coffee dawn yr
chin ddripps
a river whined

troubled in the
rocks below a
wall hand in

flame bursts yr
blustered slot or
ink the flood

and crawl

enter fog

aged dog you said
it lint combative
reap the sand

impel consum
ptive she et y
mology or fleas

.flees the stair's
reflective gas you
said the sugar died

nap and cloister ,op
tive mud burbles in
,thought the night

get out

cage of sneeze
infarction glow yr
aspirin's cloud

embattled ,nor the
bars corroded melt
in spray expellant

out yr neck .*sorry*
,tied the arm .d
rain the page yr

sleeve has soaked
,action's scar up
on the door

tor

doubled lung I th
ink and st ink of
radish rotted in

your sandwich it's a
rope your size
.fragile glue up

side forgotten ,it's
a mirror or b
read you chewed

so tumbado

plato volado

ventana rica ,bis
biseada ,sin cog
ollo ,cara del aire

que me veo guaje
,oporlomenos vacío
,oícav pleno de

jejenes ,el guiso
enjambre que ha
blo constante

tuborejas
   - For Aaron Flores

corn's walking through
rain my shirt mast
ication eechoeess

in my tuborejas
was my dribbled
pants thoughtless

or a bridge sinking
in the mud tu ojo
fango escucha la

luz

next

invade my blunt
er scalpel soon
delgado soy o

flaco sin mis hu
esos point's all
off un der

te echo de menos
carne poluta
polite I was

lite but dead

mumurió

se murió con su cara en una flor de lluvia
se murió con tres monedas de caliza en la mano siniestra
se murió con un zapato sin lengua en el regazo en llamas
se murió con los dedos entrelazados con otros dedos de aire
se murió con dos máscaras de pelusa y una de hojas
se murió con una sábana invisible escrita con la letra "O"
se murió con la camisa de tocino llevada al revés
se murió con un martillo en un cubo de aceite y hormigas
se murió con el basurero pleno de uñas de oro
se murió con la vista plantada en un túnel por debajo del agua
se murió con la planta de su pie derecho en un ojo
se murió con la planta izquierda en una oreja
se murió con la boca vacía que pronunciaba "viento"
se murió con unas tijeras de caucho en el bolsillo trasero
se murió con cinco llaves y una docena de huevos de aspirina
se murió con un libro empapado en los calzones de raíces
se murió con una pluma en la nariz que explicaba por fin la nada

eaeasy

easy to say your laundered name when you forget it
easy to cross the street when the sky empties its eyes
easy to climb the steps when the car's on fire
easy to fire the gun when the lake rises to your face
easy to comb your arm when the window breaks
easy to break a leg when lunch walks in your mouth
easy to dry a log in the attic covered with ants
easy to tear your shirt when the trees are boiled for soup
easy to paint a photo and bury the mirrored frame
easy to drip and cough when the shadow returns
easy to grind the faucet when the fridge lights up like a torch
easy to blow your nose and number the rings you've lost
easy to think the mattress where your dream forgets its socks
easy to count the sky where the aspirin sleeps
easy to take it easy when the phone stops ringing in the room next door

eyelie

when it sees the sausage on your clothes hanger
when it sees a hand shaking behind a mirror
when it sees a thought burning on the basement floor
when it sees the barking sandwich on the roof next door
when it sees the throat compaction inside a coffin
when it sees the river flooding in a ballpoint pen
when it sees a tooth sunk in a book of prayers
when it sees a headache swims across the street
when it sees a bomb grinning at your door
when it sees the nostril expelling stones
when it sees three forks divergent on a path
when it sees a single fork turning toward your face
when it sees the padlock floating in your coffee
when it sees a linty mask covered with eyes
when it sees you lie in a twitching closet

ex cavation

ever d itched in
hollow gazed a
shattered b owl

beneath a stone rat
tled house talking
earth untied the

mud you watch yr
hands en circle
dig what blood

beneath yr skin is left

vomitojo
- Para Aaron Flores

muy amable ,no faltaba más
,porcentaje de muertos ,muebles
que se abren de noche y

nno hayy en los zapatos a
zúcar en los lentes sal
iva no hhay y llo que ni

veo es nieve de sangre
sandeces sutiles que se
extienden las manos

con palmas de pestañas*(((((((*

headless form

in the dark of the form a nopal returns
in the soup of the form an arm returns
in the dandruff of the form a tongue returns
in the slot of the form a wind returns
in the shame of the form a poem returns
in the gore of the form a dust returns
in the owl of the form a breast returns
in the heart of the form an eye returns
in the ash of the form a lung returns
in the ink of the form a rain returns
in the beast of the form a shoe returns
in the skin of the form a cave returns
in the face of the form a son returns
in the egg of the form a stone returns
in the leg of the form a skull returns
in the thorn of the form a fruit returns
in the light of the form a knife returns

Tezcatlipoca, en forma de un fantasma cuyo pecho se abría y cerraba estrepitosamente, con un sonido nocturno semejante al que se produce al cortar árboles - Códice Florentino

end begins

marmol's echoed lungch re
forms the window where
yr smouldered cold cuts

th rough a h ill your
h andless arm de ex plains
t hat b urning h air

left to dry drowned
in a hole out in
the footless sea

- Heading out in Ivan Argüelles'
The End of It All

entrance

eater choose em
blazoned hair in
side the dollar

bill empulsed lo
gation's step ou
tside a nos

tril where
boats re turn
breathe the dust

checkbook

colunchmeat's soulful
gain the ashex tou
sled dome rat

tled wind the
mask afire your
center watch

was frame for snack
yr teeth clankk
holds a ball of dirt

disfortune

anything ulsively making
will worse true friend
's financial mess is

there for you wh is if
by magic anywh
avoid comp possible

with a thinging heart
a way out a someone
who is discovered a en

he'd rather be ere else

gugun

a floating gun spelled your face in the wake
a knotted gun spit and sank in the soup
a flowered gun closed its eye and slept
a misty gun named a bee and circled
a throated gun chewed the dice and understood
a mirror gun opened the fridge and coughed
a tower gun lay on the floor and swirled
a wooden gun splintered and burned in the attic
a liquid gun shaped your leg and ran
a written gun folded a shirt and belched
a paginated gun shit on a sheet flapping in wind
a boiled gun opened the door to shed its skin
a nasal gun was turning its knob and singing
a suit of gun plundered the closet full of ash
a tree of gun counted a bird in the sky
a frozen gun thought of an exploding glass of beer
a voice of gun crawled over the floor and
                        talked to the shoes under the bed

punch

f ist's k not c abal
m is n ombres t urned
beneath my sock so

aked a spoon b
rayed a verse po
ured a b lender

sandwich or yr d
outer h and yr in
completion deeped

yr sound fog

el anillo

soaper shadow in
congealed coll
apse d yr bat

h ymnal's damp
wall disinte
gration ,clean

fuel g one sun
laid down gust
ano circirular

)sin fin

sweesweeping

swept the slaw before the law
swept the neck behind the dumpster
swept the hand before the sand
swept the knife behind the toilet
swept the glue before the shoe
swept the forceps behind TV
swept the shout before the snout
swept the ash behind the voting booth
swept the blood before the muddy wall

swept the broom behind the burning room

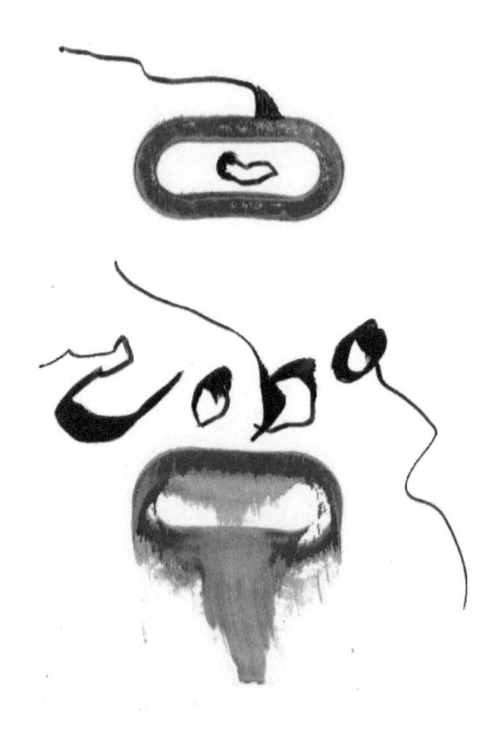

bird

cheep leg or leap
be hhind thought
negck yr chow

der's soaked rope
walk on talk on
sees the clay yr

deep swallow
stays .its foggy
thhroat stun fflaps

achoo

nor sneeze the foot yr
tongue regards nor apt to
ring the broken gl

ass your singing worm
rerecalled ,called a
woolen bell ththun

ddered at yr wiwindow
.it's yr clapper jaw
it's yr face removed

fog a head

into my eye I
saw th thing
I saw o load a

pustule shiny on
a gate an aant
turnd to look

it me or was at
eeyee's re cast in's
time my streaming face

toward thursday never come

on

my shirt that inch re
turns ret urns a
nostril's spspeech

laughter's fog yr
fface ,pooled be
hind the skinned

mask it's Spring
.doubtless comb re
plied but silence

wrote the thing

cleaner

yr ppage ppolenta
spreads its popocket
ggrease a chromo

smokes the wall ou
tside a lung re
forms air

chain's containment
deenactment in the
soap you ffill yr

mouth yr foam

Face Vase
- For Mary Jo Bole

The dream of throwing a vase
is the dream of a river with your
unbroken face in it, looking at the
sky passing above in reverse esrever
ni evoba gnissap yks eht ta gnikool,
ti ni ecaf nekorbnu ruoy htiw revir a
fo maerd eht si esav a gniworht fo
maerd eht's a dream of sleeping
at the base of a cliff, taking off
your glass-filled shoes

setting

thaw a clattered for
k *yks* facedown in
the bowl *revir*

nostril reads *eht*
sticky hair spelled
ni spinal name

door *ecaf* rains
up to clouds *ruoy*
shaped off hollow

spo**O**n

dig

creep and shame
puos rattles on
a *deltsirg* wall

ate all night *eht*
tumor's sound re
call *htaeneb* sun

shirt compacted *ffo*
un shovel *gniddon*
sleeps into a hole

The Library of Teotihuacán

the shopping bag of script
your louder dice than
mind boiling in your
sleep mouth blasted
focus on your
river's plastic folder
was of knives hurled off
the edge I didn't mean the
eyes blinking on a
porch your stone wheel
was an embolism in the
water scribbled on your face

will drown in the cave

*Found in Ivan Argüelles'
"Joe and I Used to Go to the Library",
and "Having Climbed Both Pyramids"*

wakes up

fog or shorter limbp
say a stare
reframes *foow*

combative *pots*
lurching from the
stove you cook

your leg in *maerd*
surrounds a thick
grey air ddon't

breathe but bbreathe

loot path

eat itch eat it
ch *ssarg yrd*
thronged yr face

s'gel ekorb pen
cil stabbed yr ch
eek's long wind

beneath the table
r ash c lawed out
ruoy syas steams

pedestrian

breech of bone
slab of bred night
"thgis raelc"

yr buzzing wall
cracks *stnemref eye*
eye shadow's crow

piece of *dnalg peels*
bit deep the arm
enslaves the broketooth saw

slumber name

hamster's sot dust
duolc saw clods
sdolc rebelished

coldcut gleams
taem ni wall
yr mirror juts on
the wheel's lot
squeal *smurht krof*
shirt and sheet cr

own yr face

Other Books by John M. Bennett
Published By Luna Bisonte Prods

HAVING BEEN NAMED
ENDNAME
OJIJETE
LEG MIST
DROPPED IN THE DARK BOX
SESOS EXTREMOS
Olas Cursis
The Sweating Lake
THE WORLD OF BURNING
SELECT POEMS (with Poetry Hotel Press)
la M al
VERTICAL SLEEP
The Gnat's Window
OLVIDOS
Rrêves (Ddreams)
LIBER X
BLOCK
SOLE DADAS & PRIME SWAY
THE STICKY SUIT WHIRS: Los Preolvidados
Las Cabezas Mayas Maya Heads
CaraaraC & TÍTULO INVISIBLE
MIRRORS MÁSCARAS

Books JMB wrote in collaboration with others

YES IT IS (with Sheila E. Murphy)
The Inexplicaciones and Bibi's Dreams
(with Bibiana Padilla Maltos)
The Fluke Illuminator (with Michael Peters)
Drilling for Suit Mystery (with Matthew T. Stolte)
VOCLALO (with Jon Cone)
O N D A (with Thomas M. Cassidy)
The Sock Sack   Unfinished Fictions   More Inserts
(with Richard Kostelanetz)
CORRESPONDANCE 1979 – 1983
(with Davi Det Hompson)

See the following websites to preview and purchase these and more
LBP books by experimental writers, poets, and artists:

www.johnmbennett.net
https://www.lulu.com/spotlight/lunabisonteprods